What Can We Do About OIL SPILLS AND OCEAN POLLUTION?

David J. Jakubiak

PowerKiDS press.

New York

This book is dedicated to Makayla Kuehn, whose love of the natural world and work to improve our planet's health is an inspiration.

Published in 2012 by The Rosen Publishing Group, Inc.
29 East 21st Street, New York, NY 10010

Copyright © 2012 by The Rosen Publishing Group, Inc.

First Edition

Editor: Amelie von Zumbusch
Book Design: Kate Laczynski
Layout Design: Julio Gil

Photo Credits: Cover Spencer Platt/Getty Images; pp. 4, 6, 8, 12, 18 Shutterstock.com; p. 10 Doug Armand/Getty Images; p. 14 Win McNamee/Getty Images; p. 16 AFP/Getty Images; p. 20 Saul Loeb/AFP/Getty Images.

Library of Congress Cataloging-in-Publication Data

Jakubiak, David J.
 What can we do about oil spills and ocean pollution? / by David J. Jakubiak. — 1st ed.
    p. cm. — (Protecting our planet)
 ISBN 978-1-4488-4982-6 (library binding) — ISBN 978-1-4488-5112-6 (pbk.) —
ISBN 978-1-4488-5113-3 (6-pack)
 1. Oil spills—Prevention—Juvenile literature. 2. Marine pollution—Juvenile literature. I. Title.
 GC1090.J35 2012
 363.738'27—dc22

                                              2010047319

Manufactured in the United States of America

CPSIA Compliance Information: Batch #WS11PK: For Further Information contact Rosen Publishing, New York, New York at 1-800-237-9932

CONTENTS

These workers are cleaning up oil on the beach at Perdido Pass, Alabama. The oil came from the Deepwater Horizon spill.

Trouble in the Water

On April 20, 2010, a huge blast sank the Deepwater Horizon. The Deepwater Horizon was a giant deck of machines called an **oil rig**. Workers on it helped draw oil up from deep under the Gulf of Mexico. Over the next few months, enough oil to fill more than 27,000 tractor trailer tanks poured into the water. The oil killed fish, sea turtles, and other sea animals. It washed up on beaches along the Gulf.

Oil spills cause many problems. They are just one kind of ocean pollution, though. Trash people throw into the water is also ocean pollution. Dirty water that flows into oceans after storms is pollution, too.

Oceans are homes to thousands of kinds of fish. The fish on the left is a spotted eagle ray. On the right is a threadfin butterfly fish.

Oceans Are Important

Oceans cover most of Earth. They are home to many animals, from tiny shrimp to giant whales. Sharks, dolphins, walruses, lobsters, and octopuses all live in oceans.

Many people eat food, such as fish, that comes from oceans. People go swimming, boating, and surfing in oceans, too.

Oceans even help us breathe! Earth's oceans are full of tiny living things, called **algae**. Algae take in a gas called **carbon dioxide** to make food. When they make food, they also make another gas, called **oxygen**. Algae release the oxygen into the air. People and other animals must breathe in oxygen to live. Half of the oxygen in the air we breathe comes from ocean algae.

Some of the trash dumped in oceans washes up on beaches or along rocky coastlines. Trash also gets caught in ocean currents.

In 1931, New Jersey asked the U.S. Supreme Court to make New York City stop dumping trash in the Atlantic Ocean. The city's trash was washing up on New Jersey's beaches. The Court told New York City to find a new place for its trash. Today many places have laws against dumping trash in oceans.

However, trash still makes its way into oceans. Trash from land may wash into rivers. The rivers flow into oceans, carrying trash with them. Today, a giant **garbage patch** floats in the Pacific Ocean. It has many tiny pieces of plastic, plastic water bottles, and fishing nets in it.

DID YOU KNOW?

In January 1992, 29,000 rubber ducks, turtles, and frogs fell from a ship in the Pacific Ocean. They later washed up on beaches from Alaska to Japan and England to Maine!

You can see the oil leaking from this tanker. There are fewer oil spills from tankers now than there were in the past, but they are still a problem.

How Oil Gets Spilled

Many things can cause oil spills. Oil can push through the ocean floor naturally. However, people cause most harmful spills. Ships carrying oil sometimes crash or leak. The **pipelines** that people use to move oil across long distances can leak.

In 1989, the *Exxon Valdez* was carrying oil when it ran aground in Alaska's Prince William Sound. The accident ripped open the ship's tank. Eleven million gallons (42 million l) of oil poured into the sound. The oil blanketed the water. It covered rocks along the shore. It took many years to clean the oil up. Life around the sound was changed forever.

Scientists take samples of ocean water and test them. This way they can tell if it will be safe for people to swim or fish in the water.

The Pollution You Can't See

Oil and trash are easy to see in the water. Other kinds of pollution go mostly unseen, though. For example, human waste from boats is often pumped into the ocean. When it rains, pollution from the air can fall into the ocean with the rain.

Fertilizers cause problems, too. They are used to feed plants on land. When it rains, they can wash into rivers that flow into the ocean. The extra food makes algae in the ocean grow quickly. This causes big masses of algae called **algal blooms** to form. Algal blooms can kill fish and make shellfish unsafe to eat.

DID YOU KNOW?

Oysters can eat some of the things that cause pollution in oceans. In some places, people use oysters to clean ocean water.

This brown pelican got covered in oil from the Deepwater Horizon oil spill,

Pollution is a danger to everything that lives in the ocean. Sea turtles choke on plastic bags. They eat these bags because they look like the jellyfish that the turtles often eat. Sea turtles, sea otters, seals, and whales all get stuck in old fishing nets. Birds that get covered in oil from oil spills cannot fly.

Unseen **chemicals** in oceans build up in fish. The chemicals also build up in the animals that eat fish. These chemicals often build up over a long time. In 2007, scientists in Canada found chemicals that had not been used in over 20 years in beluga whales.

DID YOU KNOW?

Waste from sick cats washes into the ocean off of California and gets into clams. Sea otters eat these clams, get sick, and sometimes even die.

This little girl is being given a piece of bluefin tuna. Tuna is yummy, but certain kinds of tuna are unsafe for young kids to eat very often.

Ocean pollution hurts people, too. Pollution has made some kinds of fish unsafe for young kids to eat. People who eat clams dug up during an algal bloom can get very sick. Swordfish, tilefish, and shark have a lot of the metal mercury in them. It is unsafe to eat these fish every day. The same chemicals found in beluga whales can be found in some kinds of fish people eat.

After the Deepwater Horizon spill, much of the fish and shrimp people caught in the Gulf of Mexico was not safe to eat. Many fishermen lost their jobs. When oil washed up on beaches, people did not want to go on vacation there. Hotels and restaurants along the Gulf coast lost lots of money.

Salt marshes help clean up pollution in the water. This salt marsh is near

Fighting Pollution

People around the world are taking steps to stop ocean pollution. Many towns along beaches have rules about what can be used to make roads. They build roads that keep all the rain from flowing straight into the ocean. Communities are planting wetlands with plants that can clean water before it gets to the oceans.

In some places, people have passed laws to keep our oceans safe. There are rules about dumping trash into the sea. Some chemicals that caused big problems can no longer be used. People are working hard to make sure that accidents like the Deepwater Horizon spill do not happen again.

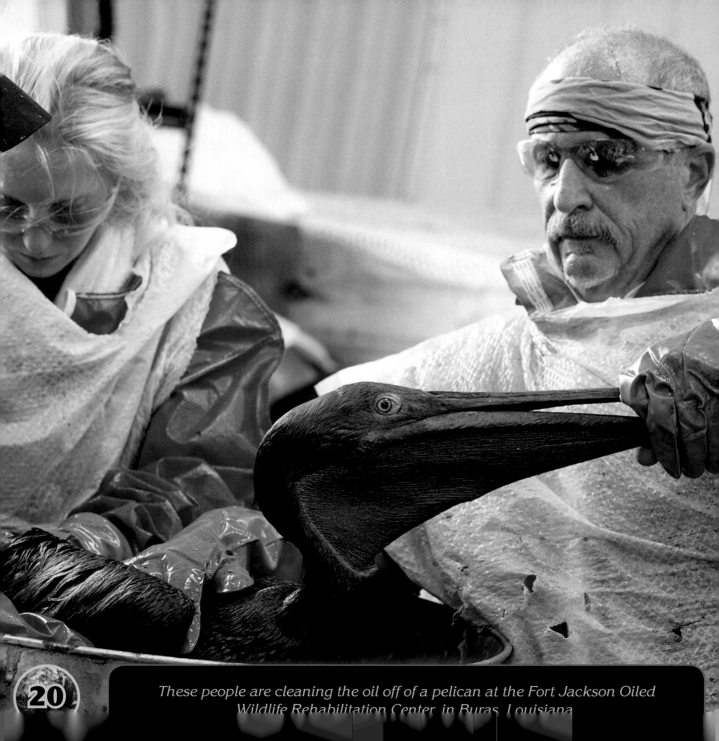

20

These people are cleaning the oil off of a pelican at the Fort Jackson Oiled Wildlife Rehabilitation Center in Buras, Louisiana.

Oil Spill Cleanups

It takes many people working together to clean up an oil spill. People use large machines to suck up oil that is floating on the water. They lay long tubes, called **booms**, around the spilled oil. Booms are stuffed with hair or other matter. They soak up oil and stop it from reaching the beach.

Chemicals are sometimes used to break up the oil. Scientists have even brought in tiny living things called **microbes** that can eat oil.

People also help oil-covered animals. They wash them with soap. They bring sick animals to **veterinarians**, zoos, and wildlife centers. There, the animals are treated and can get better.

Doing Your Part

Kids can help keep the ocean safe from pollution. One step is to make less trash. Find a water bottle you can use again and again. Use cloth napkins instead of paper napkins. Always pick up your trash when you visit the beach. Help out at cleanup days along nearby beaches and rivers. These are events at which people pick up trash. Maybe your class or club can be part of the day.

Do your part to stop unseen pollution. Cars cause air pollution that can make its way into the ocean. Talk with your parents about going some places by bicycle instead. We can all play a part in stopping ocean pollution!

GLOSSARY

algae (AL-jee) Plantlike living things without roots or stems that live in water.

algal blooms (AL-gul BLOOMZ) Huge masses of algae in one place.

booms (BOOMZ) Long, floating things that are used to keep oil spills from spreading.

carbon dioxide (KAR-bin dy-OK-syd) An odorless, colorless gas. People breathe out carbon dioxide.

chemicals (KEH-mih-kulz) Matter that can be mixed with other matter to cause changes.

fertilizers (FUR-tuh-lyz-erz) Things put in soil to help crops grow.

garbage patch (GAR-bij PACH) A large mass of things that were thrown away.

microbes (MY-krohbz) Very tiny living things.

oil rig (OY-ul RIG) A deck from which people drill for oil.

oxygen (OK-sih-jen) A gas that has no color or taste and is necessary for people and animals to breathe.

pipelines (PYP-lynz) Long lines of pipes that are used to move oil from one place to another.

veterinarians (veh-tuh-ruh-NER-ee-unz) Doctors who treat animals.

INDEX

WEB SITES

Due to the changing nature of Internet links, PowerKids Press has developed an online list of Web sites related to the subject of this book. This site is updated regularly. Please use this link to access the list:
www.powerkidslinks.com/pop/oilspill/